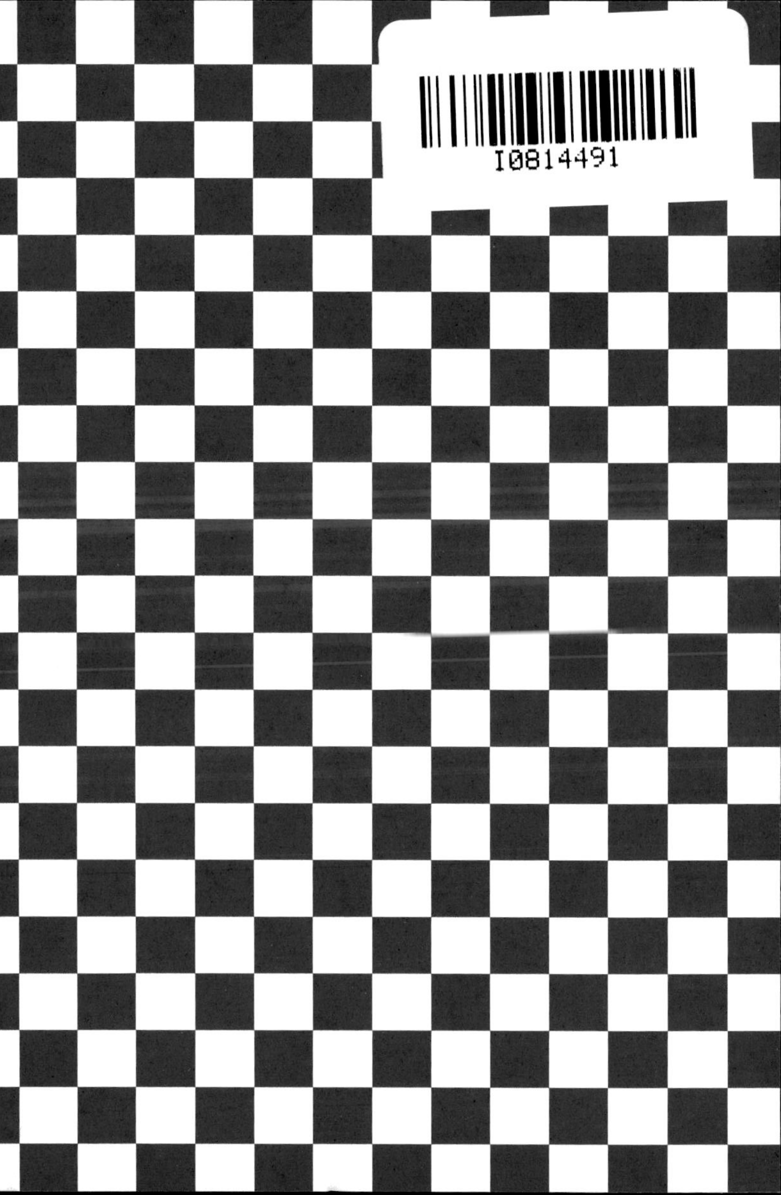
I0814491

THE POCKET DISCOVER NEW YORK

G:

Published in 2026
by Gemini Gift Books
Part of Gemini Books Group

Based in Woodbridge and London

Marine House, Tide Mill Way,
Woodbridge, Suffolk IP12 1AP
United Kingdom

www.geminibooks.com

Part of the Gemini Pockets series

Text by Becky Freeth

Cover illustration by Grace Helmer

ISBN 978-1-80247-350-6

 A CIP catalogue record for this book is available from the British Library.

Manufacturer's EU Representative: Eurolink Compliance Limited, 25 Herbert Place, Dublin, D02 AY86, Republic of Ireland.
admin@eurolinkeurope.Ie

Printed in China

10 9 8 7 6 5 4 3 2 1

Picture credits: Freepix: 4, 44, 48, 58, 59, 104, 109. Shutterstock: 6, 15, 32, 55, 56, 79 / NatalyLad; 11 / Bankrx; 13, 42, 54, 65, 82, 86, 102, 110, 116 / JosepPerianes; 16 / Bardocz Peter; 19, 92 / Vector pro; 26, 36 / Evgeniya Pautova; 47 / Tanya Lapidus; 76 / Yulya Vladson; 80 / nikiteev_konstantin; 100, 101 / netsign33; 122 / Odin Illustration.

THE POCKET

DISCOVER NEW YORK

G:

CONTENTS

WELCOME TO NEW YORK

Let's hear it for New York. A city so tightly packed with cultural landmarks that people come back year after year and still have icons left on the bucket list.

Everyone knows the highlights: Statue of Liberty, Empire State Building, Broadway and Times Square. But do you *really* know them? Like, how many windows are in the tallest building (hint: it's over 10,000), and why are there so many skyscrapers?

With this pocket guide to NYC, you can hit the ground running – like a true New Yorker – to squeeze everything you can out of a "New York Minute".

"New York is not a city, it's a world."

Truman Capote, *Breakfast at Tiffany's* (1958)

New York Neighbourhoods

Know your Soho from your Noho? You'll need these neighbourhood acronyms for your next ride in a yellow taxicab.

DUMBO	Down Under Manhattan Bridge Overpass (Brooklyn)
FiDi	Financial District
LES	Lower East Side
MSG	Madison Square Gardens
NoHo	North of Houston Street
Nolita	North of Little Italy
NoMad	North of Madison Park
NYC	New York City
Soho	South of Houston Street
Tribeca	Triangle below Canal Street
UES	Upper East Side
UWS	Upper West Side
WTC	World Trade Center

UPPER MANHATTAN

HIGHLIGHTS

The Met
Guggenheim
Central Park
Lincoln Center
American Museum of Natural History
Apollo Theater

AREAS TO EXPLORE

Upper East Side, Upper West Side, Harlem, Washington Heights

FREE EXPERIENCES

- Go window shopping along Madison, Fifth and Park Avenues.
- Pick one of the many walking routes in Central Park.
- Admire Harlem art along Graffiti Hall of Fame Way – officially renamed in 2024.
- Pay homage to John Lennon at the Strawberry Fields memorial.

MIDTOWN

HIGHLIGHTS

Empire State Building
Chrysler Building
Metropolitan Museum of Art
Hudson Yards
Times Square
Flatiron Building
Chelsea Market

AREAS TO EXPLORE

Hell's Kitchen, Chelsea, Midtown East, Theater District, Flatiron District

FREE EXPERIENCES

- Read at New York Public Library.
- Skate at Bryant Park, the city's only free-admission winter ice rink.
- Admire the architecture at Grand Central Terminal.
- Take a selfie in Times Square.
- Climb a complex network of staircases at The Vessel.
- Take in some theatre history at the Museum of Broadway.
- Amble along the High Line.

LOWER MANHATTAN

HIGHLIGHTS

Statue of Liberty
Ellis Island
Brooklyn Bridge
Top of The Rock
Little Italy
Chinatown
One World Observatory

AREAS TO EXPLORE

Lower East Side, Greenwich Village, East Village, Tribeca, Soho, Noho, Nolita, Financial District

FREE EXPERIENCES

- Ride the Staten Island Ferry through New York Harbor.
- Enter and explore what's on offer at Rockefeller Center.
- Cross over to Brooklyn and see the Manhattan skyline from the bridge.
- Walk through Wall Street and pose with the *Charging Bull* monument.

Avenues, Streets & Blocks

The boroughs operate on a handy grid system where avenues intersect with numbered streets to create a series of blocks. Of the most famous, Park Avenue includes premium real estate known as "Billionaire's Row"; and Wall Street is the home of the New York Stock Exchange. The design was an easy way to organize, build on and sell off parts of the city after the American Revolution, and contributed to the city's rapid growth into the cultural behemoth it is today.

"New York is a city of possibility and endless exploration. There's always something new to discover around every corner."

Elizabeth Gilbert, *Eat Pray Love* (2006)

THE OUTER BOROUGHS

Manhattan is just one of the five boroughs of New York City. Discover what's just across the water.

AREAS TO EXPLORE

Brooklyn, Queens, Staten Island, the Bronx

HIGHLIGHTS

- ❋ Brooklyn Botanic Garden
- ❋ Prospect Park, Brooklyn
- ❋ Brooklyn Museum
- ❋ Brooklyn Heights Historic District
- ❋ Williamsburg nightlife, Brooklyn
- ❋ Rockaway Beach, Queens
- ❋ Staten Island Zoo
- ❋ Postcards, Staten Island 9/11 Memorial
- ❋ Yankee Stadium, Bronx
- ❋ The Bronx Zoo
- ❋ New York Botanical Garden, Bronx
- ❋ Bronx Children's Museum

"There is no place like [New York], no place within an atom of its glory, pride and exultancy."

Walt Whitman (1819–1892)

New York, New York: So good they named it twice

The City of New York (in the State of New York) was called "New Amsterdam" until it was captured by the English in 1664 and renamed after King Charles II's brother, James, Duke of York. Lower Manhattan was originally a Dutch colony which they purchased from Indians of Algonquian. According to legend, it was acquired for as little as $24 (£18.50).

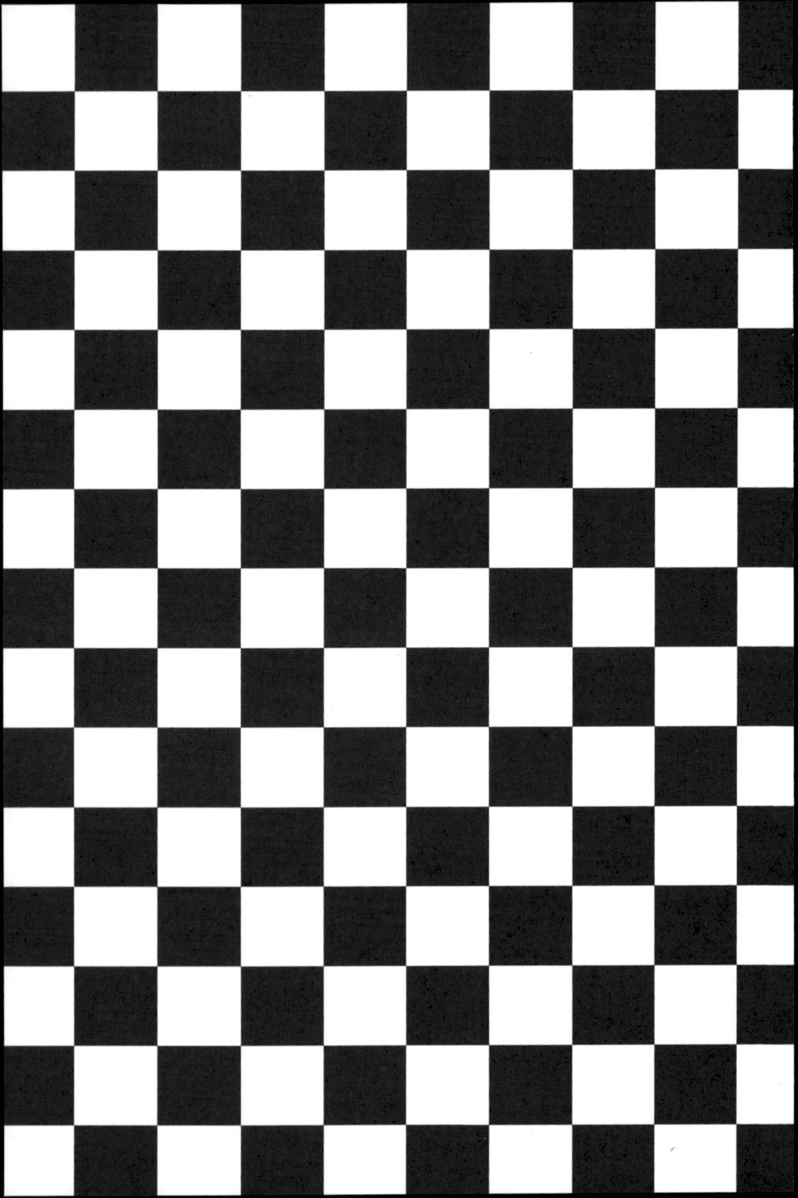

CHAPTER ONE

SIGHT-SEEING

The Big Apple

Have you heard that horse racing was to thank for New York's sweet nickname, the Big Apple?

Race days that took place here in the early 1920s were so prestigious that, for a prized horse, winning them was like biting the biggest apple.

Sportswriter John J. Fitz Gerald coined the phrase in his weekly racing column for the *New York Morning Telegraph*.

"There are many apples on the tree, but when you pick New York City, you pick the Big Apple."

John J. Fitz Gerald,
New York Morning Telegraph (1920s)

Empire State Building

BEST FOR: THE BUCKET LIST
AREA: FIFTH AVENUE

Don't Miss... The open-air observatory on the 86th floor.

Did You Know...? The building has its own ZIP code.

Insider Tip... The last elevator to the 102nd floor leaves at 1.15 am (but it'll get you there in just over 60 seconds).

No matter where you are in the city, you can expect to see the Empire State Building, the iconic Art Deco skyscraper that's dominated the NYC skyline since 1931.

At an incredible 1,250 feet (381 metres), it was the city's tallest building for four decades after completion - and with a viewing platform 102 floors above the ground, it's still one of the best places to admire the city from above.

To put its magnitude into perspective, the building even made the mighty King Kong (approximately 50-foot tall) look small when he scaled the skyscraper for refuge in the 1933 film.

There are 12,000 windows in One World Trade Center that need cleaning three times a year.

The city is home to more than 7,000 completed high-rise buildings of at least 115 feet (35 metres).

Since 1890, ten of the buildings in New York City have held the title of "Tallest In The World".

Iconic Skyscrapers You (Literally) Can't Miss

One World Trade Center (2014)	1,776 ft (541 m)
Central Park Tower (2020)	1,550 ft (472 m)
Steinway Tower (2021)	1,428 ft (435 m)
One Vanderbilt (2020)	1,401 ft (427 m)
432 Park Avenue (2015)	1,397 ft (426 m)
270 Park Avenue (2025)	1,389 ft (423 m)
30 Hudson Yards (2019)	1,296 ft (395 m)

Built pre-1950s

Empire State Building (1931)	1,250 ft (381 m)
Chrysler Building (1930)	1,046 ft (319 m)
30 Rockefeller Plaza (1933)	850 ft (259 m)
Woolworth Building (1913)	792 ft (241 m)
Flatiron Building (1902)	285 ft (86 m)

Best observation decks

The Empire State Building
360-degree views from the 102nd floor.

Top of the Rock
Clear views of Central Park from 30 Rockefeller Plaza.

Edge
Suspended in mid-air out of 30 Hudson Yards, the outdoor sky deck is the city's tallest.

One World Observatory (OWO)
Perfect views of the harbour and Statue of Liberty from One World Trade Center.

Solid Foundations

It's no coincidence that New York has become "skyscraper city" over the last 100 years.

Since square footage was not enough to keep up with the popularity of this financial, cultural and business hub, the only way was up.

The reason they were able to build such heavy buildings so high into the sky was thanks to the hard bedrock that NYC sits on.

Statue of Liberty

BEST FOR: SELFIES
AREA: LIBERTY ISLAND

Don't Miss... The official museum for photographs, videos and stories behind the largest metal statue ever constructed.

Did You Know...? The framework was made by Gustave Eiffel, the famous engineer behind Paris' Eiffel Tower.

Insider Tip... The statue is only accessible by ferry, and advance booking is recommended.

There's no greater symbol of America's freedom and independence than the Statue of Liberty.

Lady Liberty, as she is affectionately known, was a gift from France on the 100th anniversary of the US declaration of independence in 1876, and she's been guiding arrivals to the US with her 24-carat gold beacon ever since.

The details of the copper statue signify that everyone is welcome in New York, like the seven spikes of her crown for each continent of the world. Climb the 354 steps to the top and you will share her unique vantage point over the harbour.

Welcome to Ellis Island

Just a stone's throw from Liberty Island is Ellis Island, which was built in 1892 with the sole purpose of welcoming immigrants to the country. These would mainly include people from northern Europe, where times were particularly hard in the late 19th century.

In search of freedom and opportunity, roughly 12 million immigrants passed through the inspection process that was held here, involving health, wealth and welfare checks.

Of the 7.9 million who now call New York City home, over a third are believed to be immigrants. More languages - roughly 800 - are spoken here than in any other country.

"One belongs to New York instantly, one belongs to it as much in five minutes as in five years.

Thomas Wolfe, *The Web and The Rock* (1939)

Brooklyn Bridge

BEST FOR: A WALK TO REMEMBER
AREA: BROOKLYN

Don't Miss... Brooklyn Bridge Park, right underneath, by the water.

Did You Know...? A prominent and pioneering female engineer named Emily Warren Roebling was the first to bravely cross it by carriage.

Insider Tip... Time your walk with sunset to see the city light up one building at a time.

You don't have to reach dizzying heights for a panorama of the New York skyline.

Take the Brooklyn Bridge on foot to "promenade" the way New Yorkers did in 1883, when the suspension bridge (then the longest in the world) connected Manhattan to Brooklyn with a permanent footway for the first time.

The mile-long journey takes around 40 minutes, but conveniently placed benches make excellent pit stops for a breather and photo of the magnificent skyscrapers obediently clustered together on the horizon.

On 11 September 2001, two planes flew into The World Trade Center and changed New York City forever. That day, 2,606 people died as the twin towers – once the two tallest buildings in the world – collapsed to the ground.

Memorial pools opened at the site of the original towers on the 10th anniversary of the atrocity to commemorate the firefighters, American citizens and visitors who lost their lives that day.

Fittingly, the tallest building in the city today is One World Trade Center at 1,776 feet (541 metres), built in 2014 to mark the rebirth of Lower Manhattan.

9/11 Memorial & Museum

Every year, around 2.2 million people visit Ground Zero, the 14.6-acre (5.9-ha) area of New York where the towers once stood. Built in their place, the 9/11 Memorial & Museum is now one of the most-visited museums in the USA.

Through news articles, witness testimonies and photos, the museum tells the story of the day, while two peaceful commemorative pools outside are lined with the names of every person to have lost their lives in the attack.

Rockefeller Center

BEST FOR: ENTERTAINMENT
AREA: MIDTOWN

Don't Miss... The artwork, including the gilded *Prometheus* sculpture in the lower plaza.

Did You Know...? Set over three floors, the Top of the Rock observation deck gives the best view of NYC from every angle.

Insider Tip... From October, the plaza transforms into a winter wonderland, with a world-famous ice-skating rink underneath the Rockefeller Center Christmas Tree.

TV studios, restaurants, gardens and a sunken shopping mall. The Rockefeller Center is known as a city within the city.

Built in the 1930s, the 19-building complex dominates Fifth and Sixth Avenues in the heart of Midtown, and can be spotted a mile off thanks to the 70-storey art deco Comcast Building at its pinnacle.

Every morning, America wakes up to the *Today* show and, at the weekend, switches off with *Saturday Night Live*, both broadcast from the NBC headquarters here, making it feel like the cultural hub of a nation, let alone the city.

Times Square

BEST FOR: HIGH ENERGY
AREA: MIDTOWN

Don't Miss... The brand-new viewing deck called One Times Square for a birds-eye view of the action.

Did You Know...? Street level was pedestrianized in 2017, doubling the safe walking space available to visitors.

Insider Tip... Whether you visit at 2 pm or 2 am, the lights are just as bright.

No visit to NYC is complete without a trip to Times Square. Not in fact a square, but two triangles where Broadway meets Seventh Avenue, this famous intersection is a real slice of the action.

The loudest, busiest and brightest patch of "the city that never sleeps", Times Square is just as popular at midday as it is at midnight, and so bright that its LED super billboards, featuring everything from breaking news, to movie ads can be seen from space.

If that wasn't enough, it's the access point for the Theater District, where the buzzy atmosphere will put you in the mood for a show.

10 Holiday Highlights in NYC

10 Nativity scene and Christmas decorations at St Patrick's Cathedral

9 Holiday Market at Union Square

8 *The Christmas Spectacular*, starring the Rockettes, at Radio City Music Hall

7 Bank of America Winter Village at Bryant Park

6 Frost Fest at Coney Island

5 Dyker Heights Christmas Lights in Brooklyn

4 Window displays on Fifth Avenue

3 New York City Ballet's *The Nutcracker* at Lincoln Center

2 Ice skating under Rockefeller Center Christmas Tree

...1

People dream of counting down to New Year in New York at the famous Ball Drop in Times Square.

The tradition dates back to 1907, when the ball was lowered down by hand using a complex pulley system. Back then, it was illuminated by "new-fangled" electricity.

It's had several remarkable makeovers to make it what it is today: a spectacle with around a million attendees, celebrity performances, 32,256 lights and a giant disco ball glittering with 2,688 crystals.

CHAPTER TWO

PARKS & OUTDOOR SPACES

Central Park

BEST FOR: BREATHING SPACE
AREA: UPPER MANHATTAN

Don't Miss... 130 different species of animal live just yards from Fifth Avenue at Central Park Zoo.

Did You Know...? The idea for a "country park" in a busy city was the brainchild of landscape architects Frederick Law Olmsted and Calvert Vaux. It opened in 1857.

Insider Tip... Not everywhere in the park has network signal, so download maps ahead of time to avoid getting lost.

If Times Square is the beating heart of the city, then Central Park is the lungs. With 840 acres (340 ha) of trees, lawns and lakes, the space occupied by this urban oasis is bigger than the country of Monaco.

In fact, there are so many routes through the park that you could visit every weekend and never follow the same path.

Though it's not the biggest park in New York City – Pelham Bay Park, Bronx, and Greenbelt, Staten Island are both nearly double the size – it is certainly the most famous, attracting around 44 million annual visitors for walks, cycling, picnics, fitness classes and concerts.

High Line

BEST FOR: URBAN MEADOWS
AREA: CHELSEA

Don't Miss... The Chelsea Market foodhall on 15th street.

Did You Know...? Not only is this home to over 500 species of plants and 1,340 trees, you'll hear 33 species of bees buzzing happily here.

Insider Tip... For the freshest take on NYC, the High Line connects two exceedingly hip parts of town: the Meatpacking District and Hudson Yards.

Nature, art and design come together above Manhattan's West Side on the High Line.

What was once a freight rail line carrying produce across the city naturally evolved into a meadow of wild flowers after it stopped operating in the 1980s.

The disused structure was saved from demolition by Chelsea residents, and reopened in 2009, as a unique public outdoor space where manmade infrastructure meets natural grasses and trees, interspersed with art installations.

The mile-long linear garden is now so popular that eight million people walk it every year.

Bryant Park

BEST FOR: A CONVENIENT PIT STOP
AREA: 34TH STREET

Don't Miss... The occasional live magic show that takes place near the merry-go-round.

Did You Know...? The public restrooms are a landmark destination, and considered the "most luxurious" in the city after a $300,000 (£230,000) renovation.

Insider Tip... Over a million of the New York Public Library's books are preserved in temperature-controlled vaults underneath the park.

Backyards are hard to come by in Manhattan, but the New York Public Library shares its idyllic garden, Bryant Park, with everyone.

Sheltered by a canopy of trees - and skyscrapers - the busiest park in the city has manicured lawns and endless activities that you wouldn't expect to see in a thriving metropolis.

From the quaint games area with giant chess and backgammon boards to the charming merry-go-round "Le Carrousel", the park is packed with fair-weather activities. By Christmas, a free ice rink and festive markets transform the area into a winter wonderland.

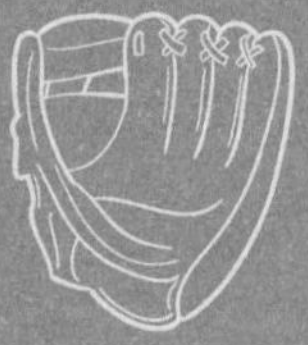

Yankee Stadium

Home of the New York Yankees, the famous Bronx baseball stadium is worth the 30-minute subway ride from Midtown Manhattan.

Most weekday afternoons, Yankee Stadium is alive with 40,000 excited fans. But the most coveted tickets of the season? Games against their NY rivals, The Mets.

On quieter days, take advantage of the unique opportunities to tour the historic stadium and on-site museum to get up close with the memorabilia of the 27-time World Champions.

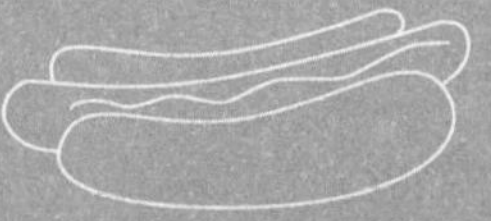

Top Dogs

On the corner of practically every block in New York you'll see a hot dog vendor – there's close to 4,000 of them.

In this city, they've been a baseball game staple since the 1890s as the fastest and most convenient way to get a taste of the Big Apple for under 20 bucks.

Want it the New York way? Top your dog with onions, mustard and ketchup.

Prospect Park

BEST FOR: OUTDOOR ACTIVITIES
AREA: BROOKLYN

Don't Miss... Ice skating in winter and roller skating in summer.

Did You Know...? The park was designated a Scenic Landmark in 1975.

Insider Tip... You can reach Lookout Hill, the highest point in the park, by steps for amazing views of South Brooklyn.

From the creators of Central Park came Brooklyn's Prospect Park just ten years later – and this, they believed, was their true masterpiece.

It housed the longest unbroken green space in the city, Long Meadow, which stretched for 90 acres. Since then, Prospect Park Zoo, Brooklyn Botanic Garden and Audubon Center at the Boathouse have arrived and increased its popularity endlessly.

In modern-day NYC, there is an endless programme of things to do here, from yoga, football and tennis on the expansive lawns to boating and fishing in Brooklyn's only freshwater lake.

Brooklyn Botanic Garden

Area: Prospect Park, Brooklyn

Established: 1911

Early proposals for a botanical garden in Brooklyn were repeatedly rejected, but the picturesque 52-acre garden is now one of the highlights of the neighbourhood.

Highlights: The first Japanese garden in an American public garden, complete with a pond, waterfall and world-renowned bonsai collection.

Best time to visit: The Cherry Blossom Festival, during late April and May.

New York Botanical Garden

Area: Bronx Park, Bronx

Established: 1891

New York's first botanic garden was modelled on London's Kew Gardens. As the city built up rapidly for business and culture, a living museum was the perfect way to preserve, research and exhibit natural beauty in a city environment.

Highlights: One million tropical, temperate and desert flora flourish in this urban jungle.

Best time to visit: The awe-inspiring Orchid Show, from February to April.

CHAPTER THREE

ARTS, CULTURE & HISTORY

Metropolitan Museum of Art (The Met)

BEST FOR: A TRIP THROUGH TIME
AREA: FIFTH AVENUE

Don't Miss... The Roof Garden, where you can look out over Central Park.

Did You Know...? This is the largest art museum in the US.

Insider Tip... Look out for live music evenings at The Met.

Its collections span 5,000 years of history, and in its century-long holding over New York, The Met has grown in size and appreciation.

Here you can travel back to Egyptian times with the greatest collection of masks, mummies and statues outside Cairo. Journey through women's fashion at the prestigious Costume Institute where *Vogue* hosts its flamboyant Met Gala in spring. And take a trip from Mexico to Peru and from Africa to Asia, exploring the most fascinating art and artefacts of the last few centuries.

Wherever The Met takes you, it is an unmissable journey.

Best Museums for History Lovers

Museum of Modern Art (MoMa)
BEST FOR: BIG-NAME ARTISTS
AREA: FIFTH & SIXTH AVENUE

Solomon R. Guggenheim Museum
BEST FOR: ARCHITECTURE & SCULPTURES
AREA: FIFTH AVENUE

New York Transit Museum
BEST FOR: TRANSPORT ENTHUSIASTS
AREA: BROOKLYN

Museum of the City of New York
BEST FOR: STORIES OF THE CITY
AREA: FIFTH AVENUE

TIP

Some museums operate a "pay-what-you-wish" scheme on certain days of the week.

The Bull, The Bear & The Wolf of Wall Street

If you liked Hollywood depictions of the city like *Working Girl* and *The Wolf of Wall Street*, a walk through America's financial epicentre is something you *have* to do when you're in town. Pound the pavements that hold so much power and responsibility, and where US flags wave from the Stock Exchange and Federal Hall.

People come for a photo with the giant *Charging Bull* statue. In the stock market, a "bear market" is when the stocks go down, the way a bear grapples at things with its paws, whereas a "bull market" represents growth, which is symbolized here by the animal raising its horns – touching the big bronze bull is thought to bring good luck.

New York Public Library

BEST FOR: PEACEFUL AFTERNOONS
AREA: FIFTH AVENUE

Don't Miss... The children's room for an appearance by the original *Winnie The Pooh* bear.

Did You Know...? The stately stone lions who guard the main entrance are known as "Patience" and "Fortitude".

Insider Tip... Free one-hour tours led by volunteers run every day except Sunday. (Sign up online.)

They say everything moves faster in a "New York minute" but inside New York Public Library time actually seems to slow down.

Not only is this the second largest library in the nation, it is the fourth biggest in the world; witnessing the 125 miles of shelving is something to behold.

In the presence of 50 million books and as many as 1,000 avid readers in the main room at any one time, the library has the characteristic throng of New York but on a much more peaceful scale.

Brooklyn Museum & Brooklyn Children's Museum

BEST FOR: RAINY DAYS WITH KIDS
AREA: CROWN HEIGHTS

Don't Miss... The fun-sized city of Brooklyn, built for interactive play inside the children's museum.

Did You Know...? In 2026, Brooklyn Museum celebrates its 200th anniversary.

Insider Tip... Brooklyn Museum is often quieter than The Met, but on a par with it thanks to the excellent exhibits.

Bring the whole family to the world's first children's museum. Founded in 1899, Brooklyn Children's Museum is an institution – it has been helping children of all ages to immerse themselves in science, history and the environment for over a century now.

It's located in the heart of the Crown Heights Historic District and only a short drive from Prospect Park, which will take you past beautiful brownstone buildings.

If you have the stamina, combine your visit with the Brooklyn Museum, one of the premier art museums in the country and an institute to rival the big names in Manhattan.

Best Things to do with Children

The city is not short of family activities, but those below are popular with adults, too.

Bronx Zoo
A must-visit attraction in Bronx Park, where Sub-Saharan warthogs cohabit with South Asian snow leopards. Fascinating.

Pier 6
A child-friendly spot at Brooklyn Bridge Park, featuring playgrounds, water play and sports courts.

New Victory Theater
New York's theatre for kids puts on shows by young performers to delight, educate and engage any audience.

FAO Schwarz
America's oldest toy store (popular with A-lister mums like Angelina Jolie and Victoria Beckham) is more like a playground.

Coney Island

From the city streets to the beach in under an hour, a trip to Brooklyn's Coney Island has enough exciting attractions (and ice cream) to feel like a retro seaside holiday in a day.

- Boardwalk and sandy beaches
- Thrilling rollercoasters
- Restaurants and cafés
- Ferris wheel
- Aquarium
- Go-karts
- Mini golf
- Gaming arcade
- Maimonides Park baseball venue

Street Art & Galleries in Chelsea

BEST FOR: CONTEMPORARY ART
AREA: WEST SIDE OF MANHATTAN

Don't Miss... Blocks 20th to 29th on the streets between 10th and 11th Avenue.

Did You Know...? The High Line starts here (or ends, depending which way you walk) and it's an art exhibition in itself.

Insider Tip... Check opening times before visiting Chelsea galleries.

The achingly cool neighbourhood of Chelsea is synonymous with contemporary art.

With nearly 400 galleries, it has the highest concentration of art spaces in one NYC locale, with the most well-known being Gagosian, David Zwirner and Marianne Boesky.

Perusing is generally free, and even though the galleries can be spread out across the neighbourhood, it's a great opportunity to appreciate the unique street art that fills in the gaps - some pieces are giant unmissable murals, but small treasures are also hidden on the sidewalks and street lamps.

American Museum of Natural History

BEST FOR: HISTORY OF OUR WORLD
AREA: UPPER WEST SIDE

Don't Miss... A glimpse beyond our planet at the Rose Center for Earth and Space.

Did You Know...? There is a butterfly sanctuary and an insectarium inside, for an up-close look at bug life.

Insider Tip... The museum has its own dedicated app that makes navigating and learning - as well as eating - on-site even easier.

Like the natural world it's dedicated to, the American Museum of Natural History has been constantly evolving.

Just three years after it was founded in 1869 - the year prior to The Met - it had outgrown its first site in Central Park. Even with 2,000,000 square foot of space today, it can only display a fraction of its 34 million artefacts at one time.

Needless to say, you can expect to dedicate at least a whole afternoon to the world's largest natural history museum. (That's if you can drag yourself away from the colossal Dinosaur Wing, the most famous part of the museum.)

Going Underground

The Subway

To connect its five boroughs, New York built a rapid transit system in 1904 called the subway - of which only 60 per cent is actually below ground.

As well as being one of the biggest city transit system in the world, with 472 stations, it operates at all hours, every day of the week, to serve "the city that never sleeps".

Steam System

Have you seen steam plume from the manhole covers in the city?

It comes from a pipe network underneath the city that uses steam to heat and cool hundreds of buildings and businesses across town.

The story of THAT Marilyn Moment

"Do you feel the breeze from the subway? Isn't it delicious!" asked the icon Marilyn Monroe as she teetered over a New York City grate on Lexington Avenue and the gust caught her cocktail dress.

Shot at predawn, it was one of the most iconic images of the 20th century. In fact, the moment caused so much commotion from onlookers that the scene, which made it into the 1954 film *The Seven Year Itch*, had to be reshot at a Hollywood film studio weeks later.

CHAPTER FOUR

SHOPPING

Fifth Avenue

BEST FOR: HIGH-END STORES
AREA: MIDTOWN

Don't Miss... Saks Fifth Avenue. The must-see flagship department store.

Did You Know...? Only one other street – Milan's Via Monte Napoleone – is more expensive than Fifth Avenue.

Insider Tip... Stop for coffee at Ralph's. Yes, Ralph Lauren.

Fifth Ave. One of the most expensive streets in retail: home to enormous flagships and designer boutiques, alike. The pinnacle of luxury shopping.

Every revered brand imaginable has a store on this iconic stretch of Manhattan, including Chanel, Tiffany & Co, Rolex and Louis Vuitton.

When you consider the location (just a stone's throw from Central Park) and the jaw-dropping architecture, it's little wonder why this iconic street attracts big-money buyers. Whether you're window shopping or on a spending spree, walking the wide boulevards can make you feel like a million dollars.

Brooklyn Flea Market

BEST FOR: BARGAINS
AREA: DUMBO

Don't Miss... Sister market Chelsea Flea if you're staying in Manhattan.

Did You Know...? *New York Times* calls the flea market "one of the great urban experiences in New York".

Insider Tip... Brooklyn Flea is open on weekends between March and December.

Brooklyn Flea is not just a chance to search out a second-hand deal, it is an experience.

Firstly, it's located under Brooklyn Bridge, ticking the boxes for picturesque and heritage. Then there's the bonus of a few great food trucks on-site or a short, post-shop walk to Time Out Food Market.

As far as shopping goes, Brooklyn Flea is *the* place to thrift unique vintage clothing or knick-knacks for the home. You can also pick up one-of-a-kind souvenirs like handmade candles or jewellery lovingly created by local vendors.

Macy's

BEST FOR: ANYTHING YOU CAN IMAGINE
AREA: MIDTOWN WEST

Don't Miss... Macy's Thanksgiving Day Parade. For 100 years now, it has signalled the start of Christmas for Americans everywhere.

Did You Know...? Macy's was the first store to be granted a liquor license after the Prohibition (see page 124).

Insider Tip... They hold as many as 300,000 pairs of shoes in the stockroom, so if your size isn't out on the shelf, it's worth asking.

Once the largest store in the world – and for a long time the biggest in the US – Macy's department store has had a lasting impact on the way we shop.

Their goods offering was pioneering in many ways. Did you know they were the first to sell multi-coloured bath towels in America? These days homewares are only 20 per cent of their bestselling stock.

Soon, their iconic red star logo popped up all over the States, but the Herald Square flagship store is still the biggest. It's so mammoth you can shop for almost anything here (homeware, luggage, fragrance or fashion), as well as dine at any one of its 11 restaurants.

Bloomingdale's

BEST FOR: LUXURY BRANDS
AREA: LEXINGTON AVENUE

Don't Miss... The iconic sound of Frank Sinatra's 'New York New York', which is played as the doors open at the start of every day.

Did You Know...? This was the first store in the US to install escalators, in 1898.

Insider Tip... Start with coffee and a muffin at the in-store Magnolia Bakery to fuel your shopping trip.

From Bergdorf Goodman to Nordstrom and Saks, when it comes to luxury department stores, shoppers are spoilt for choice in Manhattan.

"Bloomie's" is New York's best-known, not least because there are now more than 30 stores across the States. The flagship is on Lexington, another of the city's most fashionable streets.

The owners of Bloomingdale's were instrumental in bringing European fashion brands to America after World War II, and those strong ties still stand today. The store's shelves and rails are like a "who's who" of high fashion, from Vera Wang bedding to Victoria Beckham dresses.

Strand Bookstore

BEST FOR: BOOKS, BOOKS, BOOKS
AREA: EAST VILLAGE

Don't Miss... Strand merch has become almost as famous as its spine-lined shelves - pick up a signature tote for literary kudos.

Did You Know...? The bookstore featured in the *Sex & The City* TV series and the Robert Pattinson film, *Remember Me.*

Insider Tip... If in doubt, ask the staff; they are especially knowledgeable about books and even have to take a literary quiz before they're hired.

There are approximately 23 miles of old, rare and new books – that's 2.5 million – inside New York's most-visited independent book store.

Strand Bookstore is just shy of a century old, and a hotspot for visitors as well as locals: particularly famous ones, namely the late David Bowie, who considered it one of his favourite places in the city.

It used to be part of a legendary area of Manhattan called "book row", on Fourth Avenue. Where there were once 48 book shops in the 1950s, only one has survived. Instantly recognizable by its red signage, Strand has dominated the corner of East 12th Street since 1957.

CHAPTER FIVE

FOOD & DRINK

Pizza at Una Pizza Napoletana

BEST FOR: PIZZA AFICIONADOS
AREA: LOWER EAST SIDE

Don't Miss... The desserts! Save room for some gelato topped with whipped cream.

Did You Know...? NYC is typically served by the giant slice, but here you'll get smaller, Italian-style pizzettas with an inch-thick crust.

Insider Tip... They don't serve takeout, so plan your visit and make a reservation.

They used to say that you could always get a slice of pizza in New York for the same price as a subway ride. Sadly, this "Pizza Principle" no longer stands, so you have to be more selective about where you stop for a slice.

Luckily, you will find "the best pizza in the world" at Una Pizza Napoletana on the Lower East Side, which has twice topped the "50 Top Pizza" list.

Three other NYC pizza joints recently made it on the international list, including Ribalta, Don Antonio and L'Industrie Pizzeria, cementing the city's reputation for making world-renowned pizzas.

Deli Sandwiches at Alidoro

BEST FOR: FAST FOOD
AREA: SOHO

Did You Know...? Alidoro also delivers to your door.

Insider Tip... There are more than 40 sandwiches on offer and a variety of breads, so study the menu well in advance.

Don't Miss... The Pinocchio, featuring prosciutto, sweet peppers and mozzarella.

The idea of delis selling cold-cut meats and cheeses was brought to the US by European immigrants, but New Yorkers swiftly put their own stamp on things, popularizing salty grab-and-go pastrami, pickle and mustard sandwiches at affordable prices.

You can still get these no-frills New York-style "subs" on most corners of Manhattan, but sandwich shops like Alidoro prepare them with only the finest ingredients.

Since opening their first shop in SoHo in 1986, Alidoro has opened at Rockefeller Center and Bryant Park, among other prestigious locations, and is regularly rated the best sandwich shop in New York.

"New York is a great city. There is no question of that. It's such a diverse city. I've walked down the street and heard four or five different languages simultaneously. I think that's beautiful."

Patti Smith, *Marie Claire*, October 2015

The Oldest Deli in New York

Only in New York would you find a cold cut sandwich spot that's been going for nearly 140 years.

It's not just popular and consistently highly rated, Katz's Delicatessen near Manhattan's East Village was recently awarded a Michelin "Bib Gourmand" for high-quality, good-value cooking.

Hollywood really put the deli on the map back in 1989 – already a century into its tenure – when it was featured in *When Harry Met Sally* where Meg Ryan's character really, *really* enjoys her turkey sandwich...

Dinner and a Show at Ellen's Stardust Diner

BEST FOR: GUARANTEED GOOD TIMES
AREA: THEATER DISTRICT

Don't Miss... The tip bucket – to show your appreciation to the staff.

Did You Know...? Many Broadway actors started their careers as Stardust waitstaff.

Insider Tip... The line may be long but often the queue moves quickly.

Couldn't get Broadway tickets? Some say a night at Ellen's Stardust Diner – where dinner is served with a slice of entertainment – is even better than the musicals.

Once a staple of American dining culture, classic 1950s diners like this, with their neon decor and generous servings of burgers, fries and milkshakes, are a rare sight in modern-day New York. And you won't find another like Ellen's, where waitstaff working up to their big break on Broadway explode into song every few minutes.

It was the first themed restaurant in NYC and, to this day, people queue around the block for a table for breakfast, brunch or dinner.

NYC's Best Rooftop Bars

Whether you're a Martini-sipper or feeling "Cosmopolitan", New York's famous cocktails are best-served on its rooftops.

The William Vale, Brooklyn
A panorama the length of Manhattan.

Harriet's at One Hotel, Brooklyn Bridge
Drinks overlooking the East River.

Daintree, Midtown West
Unobstructed views of the Empire State.

230 Fifth, Broadway
An any-weather rooftop with heated pods.

Vintage Green, Lexington Avenue
360-degree views and a retractable roof.

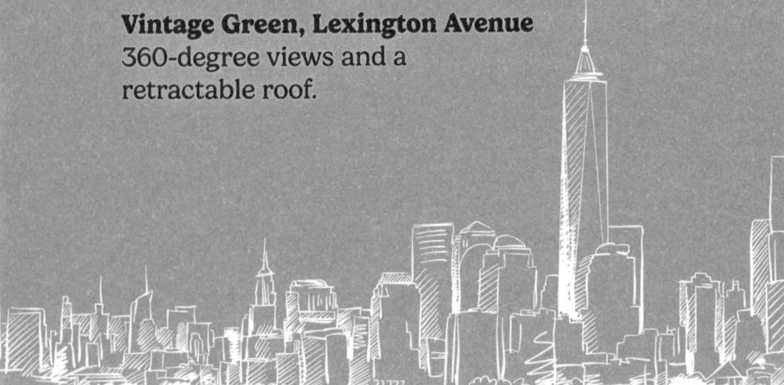

How To Make A New York "Manhattan"

The story goes that New York's most famous cocktail originated at a prominent social club on Fifth Avenue called The Manhattan Club in the early 1870s.

It's made with three ingredients - whisky, vermouth and bitters - and, according to New York's "King of Cocktails" Dale DeGroff, the secret is not to overcomplicate things. Here's his recipe:

2 tbsp (30 ml) American Rye Whisky
1 tbsp (15 ml) Dolin Dry Vermouth
1 tbsp (15 ml) Martini Ross Sweet Vermouth
A dash of bitters

Stir, then serve.

Street Food at Chelsea Market

BEST FOR: SOCIALIZING
AREA: MEATPACKING DISTRICT

Don't Miss... The doughnuts! This is a great place to enjoy a New Yorker's favourite sweet treat.

Did You Know...? The Oreo cookie was invented here when the building was The National Biscuit Company.

Insider Tip... Don't be tempted to choose the first cuisine you see – you'll get food envy as you walk around.

If there's one thing Manhattanites love, it's eating out. Unless you're Carrie Bradshaw, restaurant dining isn't an option every night, so the locals choose upmarket street food instead.

For restaurant-quality meals served as fast as this bustling city, try Chelsea Food Market, an ideal pit stop in the Meatpacking District after walking the High Line.

Whether you want a grilled cheese sandwich or lobster or ramen or gelato, the huge site which was once a biscuit factory is now a melting pot of international cuisines.

Chinatown

More Chinese people live in New York than in any other city outside Asia, and during the early days of immigration, gathering together in one neighbourhood felt more like home.

Its transformation into a cultural hybrid – with pagoda roofs on apartment buildings and lanterns hanging from fire escapes – has made it the tourist attraction it is today. Not to mention the 300 or more restaurants.

Come for the dim sum, dumplings and roast duck, but stay for the Museum of Chinese in America.

Little Italy

Rich with the culture (and cheese) of Naples and Sicily, Little Italy is a flavour of historic NYC.

It used to be highly populated with Italians and, lucky for New Yorkers, Napoletanos like Gennaro Lombardi – the owner of New York's first pizza restaurant – brought their recipes with them. Thus, Little Italy is widely considered the birthplace of New York Pizza (see page 93).

Today, as Chinatown expands, Little Italy is shrinking, but it's still the best place in NYC to enjoy authentic, handmade pasta over a checkered tablecloth.

Dessert at Eileen's Special Cheesecake

BEST FOR: CHEESECAKE LOVERS
AREA: LOWER MANHATTAN

Don't Miss... Gluten-free options, which can be prepared by special request.

Did You Know...? It all started with a "special" recipe from Eileen's late mother.

Insider Tip... Choose from a variety of finger-licking toppings - but "if it ain't broke" is your thing, go classic and plain.

Do you know what sets New York Cheesecake apart from regular cheesecake? Cream cheese. It's the ingredient that's made their desserts richer and creamier since the 1920s.

Search online for the "Best in NYC" and you'll find Eileen's Special Cheesecake, which has even made the list for the greatest cheesecake in America.

It's an old-school bakery using only the freshest ingredients, which has been making, baking and crumbing all their cheesecakes by hand for over 50 years. Queues will regularly snake out the door, patiently waiting for a taste of the famous desserts.

CHAPTER SIX

MUSIC & NIGHTLIFE

Broadway & Theater District

BEST FOR: WORLD-CLASS PERFORMANCES
AREA: MIDTOWN

Don't Miss... The shows ending their run on Broadway. They might not be back!

Did You Know...? The area is sometimes called "Great White Way" after all the bright lights and bold signage advertising the shows.

Insider Tip... Head to TKTS Ticket Booth for your last-minute tickets.

Wicked, Lion King, Hamilton, Phantom of The Opera. The most famous musical theatre shows of all time are synonymous with Broadway.

The Theater District runs from 42nd Street to 52nd Street and is lined with world-class venues, most of which popped up rapidly between 1903 and 1928.

They were built for intimate experiences of live theatre, most with decadent décor, excellent acoustics and tightly packed seating.

Even some of the biggest theatres – Gershwin and New Amsterdam – can only accommodate less than 2,000 people, so snapping up the good seats to the award-winning shows feels like winning big!

The Duplex

BEST FOR: LGBTQIA+
AREA: WEST VILLAGE

Don't Miss... The happiest hour in New York, Mondays through to Thursday.

Did You Know...? You might recognize some of the performers from Broadway.

Insider Tip... Come early for the best chance of a seat.

You're guaranteed a memorable night out at The Duplex. For those not satisfied with simply watching others belt out showtunes, this piano and cabaret bar in the heart of New York's iconic "gay-bourhood" the West Village is the place to embrace your inner performer.

Drag shows are the big draw, five nights a week, but the venue also hosts trivia nights, stand-up comedy, dancing and parties by the piano where the staff aren't just running the bar, they hold a tune, too.

Going strong in the city for 70 years now, The Duplex unites a new generation of revellers with the loyal fans who come back every time they're in town.

Stonewall
The birth of the modern LGBTQIA+ movement

When the Stonewall Inn gay bar in Greenwich Village was raided by undercover police officers on 28 June 1969, it was the spark that lit six days of fiery unrest in the city.

On the night, patrons refused to hand over their ID cards, to protect both their names and gender identities. Their arrests and unfair treatment by officers led to protests lasting nearly a week.

Thereafter, an annual demonstration took place on the last Saturday in June, which ultimately became the globally-recognized event known as Pride.

Guide To NYC Pride

The biggest queer event in the calendar is NYC Pride, from mid- to late June. The annual celebration is dedicated to highlighting, supporting and advancing LGBTQIA+ rights.

Ways to celebrate...

- March with the crowds from Fifth Avenue to the West Village.
- Wear bold colours – the brighter the better!
- Spend a day at Jacob Riis, the "Gay Beach of New York".
- Brush up on your cultural theory, fiction and poetry at Lesbian Herstory Archives.
- Visit Stonewall Inn, a National Historic Landmark dedicated to gay rights.

Madison Square Garden

BEST FOR: WITNESSING GREATNESS
AREA: MIDTOWN

Don't Miss... Sneakers, boxing gloves and tracksuits worn by the real sports legends.

Did You Know...? MSG has moved four times since it was opened as a circus in 1879.

Insider Tip... You can tour the locker rooms and backstage areas most days.

New York is not short of world-famous entertainment venues: Radio City Hall, Carnegie Hall, Gramercy Theater and Barclays Center are some of the most iconic places to see sport or live music in the city.

But then, there's Madison Square Garden. It's where Marilyn Monroe sang 'Happy Birthday' to President John F. Kennedy, where the undefeated Mohammed Ali was beaten by Joe Frazier in "The Fight of The Century", and where Elvis Presley played his only New York concerts.

Snagging tickets to see the New York Knicks or New York Rangers play at home is the ultimate way to witness history these days.

Apollo Theater

BEST FOR: SOUL
AREA: HARLEM

Don't Miss... Amateur Night, an event that's witnessed 90 years of music history.

Did You Know...? Drake and John Legend are just some of the artists who have played here in recent years.

Insider Tip... Even in the gift shop there is a lot you can learn about the history of the venue.

To enter the historic Apollo Theater in Harlem is to be in the presence of jazz, soul and blues greatness.

The black music venue launched the careers of global artists such as Ella Fitzgerald, Lauryn Hill, The Jackson 5 and James Brown, who came to this stage as newcomers on Amateur Night. It was so instrumental in Brown's success that he returned to record his chart-topping album, *Live At The Apollo*, from here.

You can still come to the Apollo for the Amateur Night talent show every week in the hope of witnessing an artist destined for future greatness.

The Bronx
Birthplace of Hip Hop

Biggie Smalls, Jay-Z, 50 Cent, Nicki Minaj, Busta Rhymes - just some of the hip hop artists and global icons who hail from New York City.

The Bronx, specifically an apartment building at 1520 Sedgwick Avenue, is believed to be where rapping, breakdancing and scratching records on turntables originated.

A guided tour of Manhattan, Harlem and the Bronx is a great way to find out more about the Apollo Theater and Rucker Park.

Best NY Pop Culture Tours

Sex & The City filming locations

Walk a mile in Carrie Bradshaw's Manolo's, from her West Village apartment to her favourite stores on Bleeker Street.

FRIENDS hangouts

Even though the sitcom about six Manhattanites was filmed in Los Angeles, explore locations that inspired the show.

The Beatles' Rock & Roll history

From the Ed Sullivan Theater where the band made their US debut to the spot where John Lennon was assassinated.

The _Gossip Girl_ story

Go behind the scenes of the Upper East Siders' charmed life, stopping by Bethesda Fountain and Chuck Bass's Empire Hotel.

Please Don't Tell

BEST FOR: AN IMMERSIVE EXPERIENCE
AREA: EAST VILLAGE

Don't Miss... The entrance! It's inside Crif Dogs, but it's unmarked and easily ignored.

Did You Know...? We call it a "Speakeasy" because the idea was to keep your voice down in these illegal bars to avoid attracting attention.

Insider Tip... Try the Waffle Chips with cheese sauce. If you know, you know.

It's been estimated that there were 32,000 speakeasies across New York by the end of the Prohibition – the criminalization of the manufacture, sale and transportation of alcoholic liquor – in 1933.

Today, there are a handful of hidden cocktail bars that still feel authentically "underground". Please Don't Tell in the East Village is one of them. You'll need to jump through a number of hoops to get in, starting with a call from a pay phone via the hot dog vendor next door. And you have to be on the list – so book in advance.

Naturally, the drinks menu here is the big draw, with an excellent selection of delicious and unusual cocktails.

Prohibition in New York

The NYC nightlife scene was forced underground during the Prohibition era of the 1920s, when the sale of alcohol was made illegal in the United States.

New Yorkers tried their best to fight the ban, protesting in the streets and writing to government to argue that it was unenforceable by local police.

Their secret stand against the law was best defined by the sheer number of illegal bars that cropped up across the city.

TIP

Look out for The Campbell, the not-so secret speakeasy at Grand Central Terminal, established in a hidden apartment upstairs in 1999.

"There is something in New York air that makes sleep useless."

Simone de Beauvoir,
America Day by Day (1948)

Final Destination
Grand Central Terminal

There aren't many transport hubs in the US that double as tourist destinations, but there's something magnetic about Grand Central.

An estimated 750,000 people pass through the building daily, yet many have nowhere better to be than admiring the grandeur of this gothic monument with its vaulted ceilings, marble floors and famous four-faced clock.

It was former First Lady Jackie Kennedy Onassis who fought to save the building from demolition in 1975, saying: "If we don't care about our past, we can't have very much hope for our future."

FACT
It's called "Terminal" not "Station" because trains start or end their journeys here, meaning none are passing through.

Getting Around Town

Honk, if You're Feeling Risky

Did you know it's illegal to hold down your horn in New York City? Offenders can face a fine of up to $2,500 (£1,900) if they're caught!

A Tip to Remember

Tipping in NYC is a big deal. It's customary to add 20 per cent to a taxicab fare, and in seated restaurants – where waitstaff take orders and bring the food to the table – expect to add between 15–20 per cent for service.

Grab a Cab

"Hail a cab" by gesturing to any yellow taxi with the medallion number on top lit up. If it's off, they're either busy or off-duty.

Jay Walking

Crossing the street outside of a crosswalk or against traffic signals was made illegal in New York in 1958, and carried a $250 fine. In November 2024, the law changed and it's now officially permitted. But, please, still proceed with care!

"The city seen from Queensboro Bridge is always the city seen for the first time. In its first wild promise of all the mystery and beauty of the world."

F. Scott Fitzgerald, *The Great Gatsby* (1925)

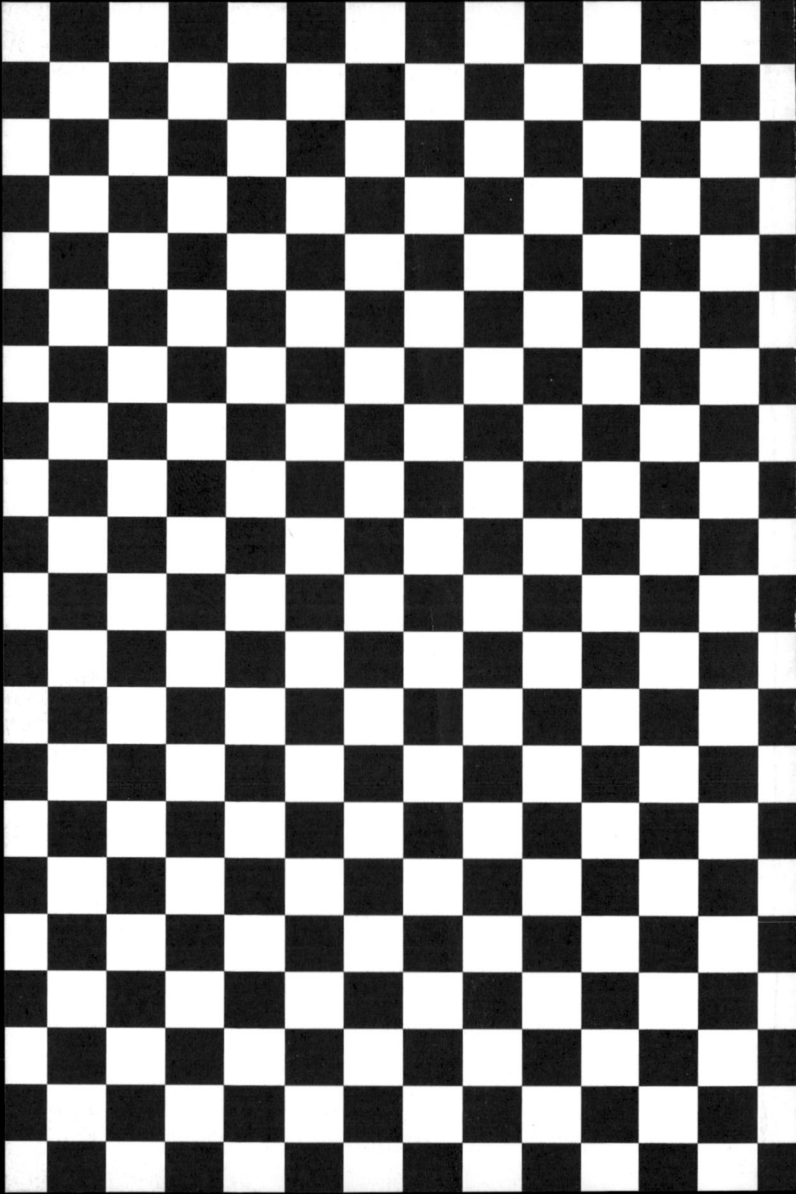